9 KEYS YOU MUST MASTER TO BE A MISERABLE ASSHOLE

or

HOW TO BE AN ASSHOLE

DENNIS WALLER

Disclaimer- Dennis Waller is not certified as a Proctologist but is considered an authority on the subject of miserable assholes and is a popular speaker to groups interested in learning more about dealing with this ever growing segment of the population.

Copyright © 2012 DENNIS WALLER

All rights reserved.

ISBN: 1479314129
ISBN-13: 978-1479314126

DEDICATION

No one is safe when it comes to the wisdom of Foghorn Leghorn, not even Roger Goodell, { see, Foghorn is a Packers Fan}. " I say that Roger Goodell is so light headed that even Ricky Williams has to look up to him. That boy has got more vacant real estate in his head than Detroit. I say he must be a Hawk, a Seahawk that is"

CONTENTS

ACKNOWLEDGMENTS

NO, THIS IS NOT MY AUTO-BIOGRAPHY, Thank You!

CHAPTER ONE-HAVING AN OVER ABUNDANCE OF SELF-IMPORTANCE

Don Juan told Carlos Castaneda that Self-Importance is man's greatest enemy. Now, I am guessing here but even a spiritual leader like Don Juan recognized that at the core and heart of every miserable asshole is an over abundance of self-importance. The first step in becoming a miserable asshole is to become self-centered and self-absorbed. Yes, self-importance is the first key!

So this is where we will start on the path to becoming a miserable asshole. This is the top of the list in characteristic traits needed for being a miserable asshole.

What is self-importance? Self-importance is like quick sand. If you continue to sink into this quick sand of self-importance, there will come a point where you will not be able to regain or to return to a normal state, much less find yourself on a spiritual path. Self-importance can almost guarantee a complete stoppage of any positive growth. At that point, you will be past the point of return.

At this stage, you'll be a 100% asshole. Maybe running for office might be your best bet. At least, if you win, you'll be among your own kind. No worries, we have managed to find a place to keep you all together. {Important fact-Federal and State capitals are sanctuary cities for miserable assholes, jerks, scum bags, dumbasses, etc.}

And if you don't win, well, you can go hang out with John Edwards or with Anthony Weiner. Remember though, don't mess with Texas, keep your photos to yourself! Yes, having too much self-importance puts you on the fast track to a most miserable life, just ask the two guys in the this paragraph.

Two other terms for self-importance that means the same thing are self-centered and self-absorbed. If you ask me, they're just words that say "asshole" in a nice way.

It helps to be unrealistic in your expectations of others. You gotta believe that since your "Albert Einstein Level" IQ is an amazingly high "86." You expect everyone you meet should have the same Einstein type IQ of 86 too. However having an IQ of 86 and being a miserable asshole makes you almost a shoe-in for public office or a CEO of

Home Depot or Microsoft or at a last resort, Wall Street or maybe the Federal Reserve.

If you know that imports come from somewhere else besides here, you're qualified! Doesn't matter if you don't know that, there are plenty of places for you to go and really screw the pooch, share holders, the sexy intern, customers, family, country, etc.

Self-importance is the pinnacle of all the goals, the brass ring for which the Ego desires to attain. When you are completely absorbed in your self-importance, your Ego is the King Asshole and Lord Douche Bag over your miserable world, and it is ecstatic, just beaming with pride!

If this is the case, you might want to consider changing your name to Dick or Bush. If you don't like those names, you can tie your dog to the top of your car and drive around instead. You'll get the same effect either way. But really try to pick a name that has something to do with screwing. And you won't need your birth certificate anymore so throw it away, after all, your above the law of the monkeys. Monkeys don't care about those things.

Or, if you're in Hollywood, look up that guy from Baywatch, David something or the other, you know who I am talking about. {Yes, any reference made to the screen star genius David Hasselhoff and his step-daughters will be remove from the German issue, don't want to start WWIII or upset Mr. K West.}

Because of your behavior, the Ego gets to run amuck. There is no low too low for your ego to attain. It is similar to the inmates running the alyssum. While being in a state of self-importance makes your life miserable, at least you have comfort in knowing that your Ego is enjoying the hell out of your misery while destroying everything around you.

The upside at this point is will you feel like the right hand of God. With this mindset, you might try to recreate the Crusades or at the very least let everyone know you have God on speed dial. This "God" complex is very common among miserable assholes, they are all throughout history.

One tell-tell sign that your Ego has taken over on the path to the Misery Kingdom is when you are breaking your own principles faster than you can lower them. Miserable people have a sliding scale of principles that change to fit the situation. Whatever or whoever you need to be at the moment, your values will adjust to accommodate the situation.

For instance, there was this miserable asshole TV Preacher reading his bible while taking a shit. Once he realized that there was no toilet paper, what do you think he used? Maybe the book of Proverbs? Here is a proverb for ya, check for toilet paper before starting your business in the outhouse Mr. Bakker.

There is never one bottle of beer or a bottle of gin too many or one girlfriend, boyfriend, or both of them at the same time too many when it is in front of you. Unless you're Hugh Grant, then we must include the TS/TG community too. Hey! I don't care what gets your flag up the pole, not my problem and don't care.

Your platform is to say no to drugs, unless someone is offering them to you for free, well, then, it's okay. That is what rehab is for, right? If you need more info, call Miss Lindsay Lohan, she is an authority on this subject, if she isn't available, talk to her mom, it runs in the family.

By the way, I will make an exception for Lindsay, I would try to make it work with her. We could try to raise the flag. Not all miserable assholes are untouchable, I'm equal opportunity here.

Of course you can play "strip pool" especially if your last name is Wales. But if you do, just make sure to take the I-phones away from everyone unless you don't care if the world sees your ass, then, by all means, go for it, after all, you have God on your side not to mention the Lizard Queen. But keep this in mind, this is America you asshole, we don't give a hoot about the royal willy here, take it back across the pond and let the Brits give a yank on the old royal dilly.

Also, it wouldn't be a bad idea to have your brother's wife wear some clothes when they are swimming, again, unless you don't care about mommy trying to get the French government to step in and managed your mistakes. Sorry Lads, you have a lot to learn.

Yes! Miserable Assholes can and do have that much power. By the way, that does make for an interesting pair, King to be Willy and his Queen Titty, I kind of like the ring of it. Least we forgot Prince Buck Silly. Maybe you boys can learn a trick or two from the master, Slick Willy. I'm sure in the end, we're the ones that 's going to get fucked silly.

Having an overabundance of being in a state of self-importance is critical in being miserable. Practicing the act of self-importance requires that you are constantly being offended by everyone and everything you come in contact with. One of your favorite sayings are, "I dare you!" or "While, I've never!" or "Don't you know who I am?"

 For instance, someone pulls into your lane on the highway, don't they know that you're driving here too," Excuse me!" Or at the store and the jerk in front of you is taking his time in paying for his items because he stops to visit to the cashier, "Hey, we are waiting here, take that crap somewhere else, no one cares about your damn dog." Geez, don't wish you could just shot them and be done with it?

Oh, how about the old lady driving in front of you in the parking lot taking her time in order to be careful while looking for a parking spot, "Hey asshole, get the hell out of the way, don't you have a funeral to go to?" And when someone has the nerve to call you out, you reply, "OMG, Really? The nerve some people have!"

One of your most used sayings is, "Don't you know who I am?" This is used anytime you feel that you are not being taken care of in the manner that you think you deserve. It is all about you and you get angry when the world doesn't stop for your whims. So in order to get the attention of the world, you put up this attitude to let the morons know that they are in the presence of your greatness, well, at least, that is your thought process. You seem to do this in the coffee shop when you are in a hurry or at the check in desk at the airport when you don't get the seating assignment that you prefer.

Patience is not a virtue of a miserable asshole. Nope, it is the opposite. You know you're an asshole when you ask where the hell is your coffee is at before the poor cashier has had time to give you back your change. Or when you cut to the front of the line and say, "Excuse me, I am in a hurry. Oh? Don't you know who I am?" Ah, all the little people in your way, you certainly know how Doctor Smith felt on Lost in Space, don't you? I betcha you have the entire series on Blue-Ray because you can sympathize with Doctor Smith for having to live among the monkeys of the world.

My favorite miserable assholes are those who go to McDonald's and asked if the tomatoes used are Biltmore tomatoes or perhaps Early Cascade? And, how years was the cheese aged before being used and if the beef is Aged Kobe Beef? It's a McDonald's you fucking ignorant asshole, what do you expect for a dollar? But you're an asshole and this is what assholes do, just keep that in mind the next time you are behind one of them.

To be fair, not only are assholes customers at McDonald's, they are also employees. You know McDonalds is an equal opportunity employer so they have to give these degenerates a job if they qualified for it by knowing what color button to push when someone orders a Big Mac.

An example of one of these assholes is when I went to a McDonalds and order a large ice tea. No problem until I noticed a frozen cricket inside one of the ice cubes. When I brought this to the attention of the idiot at the counter, they went to go get the manager. This asshole got mad and accused me of bringing in the frozen cricket in a ice cube in order to get my one dollar ice tea for free. When I reminded the asshole that I didn't bring in any frozen cricket ice cubes but thanks for the idea and by the way, does that really worked, she said to get out of the store before she called the police. Which I wouldn't have mind except the poor frozen cricket isn't so frozen anymore floating around in my tea. About this time, some poor soul received his quota of frozen crickets for the day in his coke while getting ice. Well, the asshole manager called it a conspiracy against McDonalds. This event didn't end well. In the end, I had a spokesman from McDonald's call to apologize and did ask, by the way, how was the frozen cricket, it was something the test kitchen was working on.

Now, the real question here, Are these imported or domestic crickets, because I had heard that imported crickets came from somewhere else other than here. I need to know since I was contemplating running for office and an qualified candidate needed to know these things.

Yep, in order to really be at the top of the game of self-importance, just about everyone has got to piss you off with their stupidity. It just doesn't make any sense, I mean, don't they know who you are and they had better recognize that fact? In order to really have an unhealthy amount of self-centeredness you need to lose all resemblance of compassion, humility, kindness, or any other positive emotion. An asshole's motto is, "Better to be pissed off than to be pissed on." So, when one of these miserable fucks tells you it's raining, run for cover.

In addition to that, you need to create a sense of complete separation between you and the world. In your eyes the world is nothing more than a cesspool of monkeys. You feel that you are on the planet of the apes and you are the only human among all the monkeys. { Note to monkeys, please see last chapter.}

An example of this is when some poor lady drops her bags of groceries in front of you while you are attempting to get out of the parking lot and you go, "Dumbass, what an idiot?" and honk the hell out of the horn to ensure she gets the message. And to make sure she does, you pull up next to her car, roll down your window and remind her what a stupid shit she is in case she didn't figure it out with all the honking and hand gestures, you know, just in case she is blind and deaf you know, you really to need to make sure, so there won't be a next time, right? Gotta make sure she understands who you are! Trust me, oh, she will know who you are!

Or the poor kid at the convenience store who is a nickel short on paying for his soft drink, instead of pitching in the nickel, you ridicule the poor moron for not having enough sense, literally and figuratively, to know what a soda cost, "What kind of stupid ass would go into the store without enough money?

However when you are the one that is a nickel short, it's you saying, "Hey Dumbass, Don't you know who I am? Geez, stop being an asshole and let me have my cigarette's. How in the hell can I pay for them if I'm standing here naked? You Dumbass, just give them to me!"

There is a story of a fellow standing in line to board a plane that didn't care for his setting assignment. He became an obnoxious whining "it's all about me" asshole and told the lady, "Don't You Know Who I Am?" At that point, the lady got on the mike and said, "Excuse me ladies and gentlemen, I have a white man, about six feet tall, 50 years old, about 200 pounds in a blue pinstripe suit who doesn't know who he is. Does anyone know who he is?" At the back of the line someone said, "Yeah, an asshole."

Even this embarrassment didn't faze our self-centered, self-importance kind of guy. He should serve as a poster child for all the wantabe self centered, self absorbed assholes who are in their little Self-importance stage of their life.

Remember! No matter how broke you are, no matter how little education you have if any, how many failed relationships you have had, or how pathetic your life is, everyone else is an idiot, they are all stupid, and constantly in your way, not to mention that they all are beneath you.

And, it is Never your Fault. Oh hell no, you never did anything to deserve it. It is hard living in a world where you are the only one that has a clue. It is hard having to deal with a bunch of moronic, bat shit stupid, corn flake eating dumb-asses when You are the only one that knows anything.

Self-importance has two faces, arrogance and self righteousness. The great thing about self-importance is it prevents you from growing spiritually. In order to really cultivate your self-importance you need to have a massive amount of deep insecurity, immense shame, and a knowing at the deepest levels of your soul and existence that you are an unworthy and useless piece of shit that is doing nothing but taking up space. At least, I would like for you to think that.

This is where the Ego, King of Assholes comes into play. By focusing on the external values of others, even when the perspective is wrong, the Ego will always find a way to compensate for your own short comings by tearing the people down around you to a level well below yours.

Self-righteousness requires you feel superior to everyone you know. You must also have a God complex to be self-righteous. This is common trait among Doctors. They have it down pat. There must be a course in doctor school called, "How to be an asshole." They are masters at being assholes and they serve as a good teacher if you need one.

The sad reality of self-importance is it is nothing more than an attempt to make up for your own serious fucked up issues. The sad truth of self-importance is all the stupidity you witness, all the moronic behavior, all the friction that you experience is nothing more than a mirror reflection of your own inner state of affairs. What you are truly seeing is your own insecurities, fears, loathing, and contempt being played out in front of you for you to witness. Yeah, maybe life is trying to tell you something here.

Consciously or subconsciously, you have decided to find fault in everyone you see. Your self-importance is nothing more than a mask to hide your own problems and issues. But the great thing here is the Ego blinds you from the truth so you can continue being the miserable asshole you are without ever having to know the truth. So give a great big "Thank You Ego!"

Now arrogance is a little different. It is the foundation for becoming an asshole. The more arrogance you have, the bigger the asshole you can be. I say, be all you can be and go for it! I mean if this is your goal in life, go out and be the biggest asshole you can be! If you are going to be miserable, at least have something to show for it. Just because you do everything else half ass, at least do this right.

That way when someone walks up to you and calls you an asshole, you can proudly say, "Thank You, Thank You very much! It took a lot of work to become the asshole you see standing in front of you. Thank you for recognizing and acknowledging my hard work!"

That way when you walk down the street people will turn and say, "Now there goes a real asshole." Stand tall. Walk proudly. Take pride in that comment, you've earned it,,,, you miserable asshole.

CHAPTER TWO- BLAME

What is interesting about Blame is at its core, it is the inability to accept responsibility for your actions. It is so much easier to just blame everyone and everything else than to take responsibility for your own actions. Yes, it creates misery but it takes no effort to blame people and events but it does take a lot of work to take responsibility for your actions. Playing the blame game is a notch below self-importance. You could say that if this is where you are, you haven't graduated to a full blown self absorbed miserable asshole living as if the sun waits for your call to rise.

There are two types of the blame game. Blaming others and blaming yourself. Most people who are miserable play them both. We are going to look at the first game, blaming others.

In blaming others you think you are released from responsibility. In being unable to take any responsibility for yourself, you create a treasure grove of excuses. Your entire life is centered around which excuses are you going to use for any situation. If you really wanted to do something useful, you could write a book called, "1,001 Excuses for Assholes." Now that would be something that would benefit the lot of you.

Let's look at some examples of people who play the blame game by blaming others. For the poor employee that just can't get their act together, their boss gets to hear an assortment of excuses such as,

My car wouldn't start, {but you only live three blocks away.}.

They cut off my lights and I didn't have a way to wake up, { but you have the new I-phone with all those apps.}.

I ran out of gas, {third time this week.}.

The dog was out of food, {you don't have a dog.} The cat was sick, {and?}.

I couldn't find my car keys, {really?}

I forgot about the time changing forward, {even though it happen two weeks ago.}

I forgot you told me to come in early, {this means, screw you asshole.}

I forgot I couldn't leave early yesterday, {also means, screw you asshole.}

I couldn't find a place to park, {but you take the bus to work.}

I had to go to the bank to get some money, {then why are you asking for lunch money from your co-worker?}

I had to go to the Post Office to mail the light payment, etc, etc.

As you can see, a miserable asshole living in a world of blame has an excuse for everything. Even at home, the miserable asshole has a repertoire of excuses. Let's look at a few, "Why haven't you wash the dishes?"- Because, I am letting them soak because they are really dirty and I am taking a break, I am tired from thinking about it. I mean, I filled up the sink, that is a lot of work in itself! It's not my fault. Or, I didn't dirty all those dishes so why or should I have to clean them?

"Why haven't you taken out the trash?" -Because my eye lids hurt, how am I to know what to do? nobody told me anything. Is that what that smelly pile is? I thought it was something you were saving for work. You know, save the Rain Forest from the Eskimos or something.

"Why are your clothes dirty?" -Ah?, Because I don't have any quarters? or -Oh yeah, the machine is broken, that's it, the machine is broken. Besides, they are only going to get dirty again. And there are starving children in the Bronx and I don't want to upset the delicate balance of nature. You know, Global Warming.

And there is the time tested and all around excuse to use when nothing else works, it is, " I forgot." Isn't it funny that miserable assholes seem to forget a lot? It seems in order to be a miserable asshole, you must learn to forget a lot of stuff. Yeah, "forgetting" is an important part of being a miserable asshole and a big part of playing the blame game.

For instance, "My phone doesn't work because I forgot to pay it, the phone company didn't send me a reminder" -They did, you just blew it off. ""My wife left me last night." -Wow really?, It took the dumb bitch long enough to realize what a miserable asshole you are and leave your sorry ass! My lights got cut off, I forgot to pay it."- Really?, You should have thought about that before going to the Casino and losing your pay check there on your way home. " I forgot to put gas in the car." -Was that after you bought the 12 pack of beer and a carton of cigarettes?

Or in relationships, you get busted by your wife banging the baby sitter and when she ask what about her, what do you say? I forgot! Yes, that's it, I forgot dear. It is simply an oversight of the budget committee, that's all, no worries. However to make you happy, I'll export my willy from the trade negotiations. Seems we have an unauthorized invasion of the low lands. But, for the record, I did not have sexual relations with the baby sitter as defined by the Geneva Convention. By the way, can you, for the record, define the word "sex?"

Seems that the things that really don't matter to you get forgotten about easily. It is just too easy to sit on the front porch with your cooler of ice cold beer, cigarettes and chips and just sit there complaining about being stuck cause the car is out of gas, the lights are turned off and blaming the "Man" for not giving you a break. Isn't it funny how the "Man" doesn't give two shits about you? Well, if the "I forgot" excuse doesn't work, we always have the "Man" to blame. By the way, where in the hell did that dog run off to? I'll tell ya, he got fed up with your nonsense and move on down the road along with your ex-wife.

Yes, if you desire to be a miserable asshole, you must develop a very long and a really good list of excuses to get out of taking any responsibility for anything. By blaming others for your own inability to take care of yourself, you'll be able to enjoy being a miserable asshole by having your book of excuses that are tailored made to fit the occasion.

Now, let's talk about the other side of the blame game. There must be a school somewhere for miserable assholes who play the blame game because they all have the same playbook. Let's take a look at a couple of those plays. Now, fill in the blanks,

"I can't do it because I am _____"

"I can't do it because I didn't have any _____"

"They don't give me a break because I am _____"

"They don't like me because I am too _____"

Some of the words you can use to fill in the blanks are, black, white, red, green, uneducated, untrained, fat, skinny, tall, short, old, young, a loser, stupid, ghetto, redneck, dumb, half wit, poor, etc, etc.

Another great excuse that is a "fill in the blank" is:

"I can't do it because it's too _____"

The words to choose from include, hot, cold, windy, cloudy, dusty, clear, sunny, wet, dry, hard, high, low, long, short, etc, etc.

I am sure that if you are really working on being a miserable asshole, you could add more words to the list above. There is a common thread with all of this and it is the word, "Can't." You cannot, repeat, cannot be a miserable asshole without knowing how to use the word "Can't."

As you can see, the word, "Can't" is really important. You can't get by with just excuses, you need the right words too. "Never" is another good one to use. It can be used in your excuses as well as your mission statement. Like, "I'll never get promoted, because I didn't have any _____" or my favorite, "I never get any respect because I am _____"

Yes, when blaming yourself don't forget, {now isn't that funny, we can't forget this,} to use these words: never, can't, always, everyone, every time, and so on.

Here, let me show you how to use these words to blame yourself for your pathetic miserable life, "Every time I try to do something, it fails, everyone tells me I can't do it because I am stupid, that I'll never amount to anything because I am poor, it's always the same story with me, I never get a break because I am a loser. Nobody likes me"

Now, that is working the blame game good. You got all the key words in on your statement. Hey, look, no one said that being a miserable asshole was going to be a walk in the park, Nope, Never said it would be easy. Now get out there and try out these new tricks and see if they work for you.

If you get to feeling bad realizing how really worthless you are, Rejoice! You're on the right track! Atta boy, you miserable asshole!

I like this group of miserable assholes. No matter how great something is, they always focus on the negative side of things. If you are having a great day, go find one of these guys and tell them your story. I betcha they will find stuff in that story that will have you looking for a rope and a tree.

It doesn't matter what it is, they will find the ugly truth buried in there somewhere. Take them to a restaurant and order them a steak. They'll be telling you about the cow's mother having an affair with the other bulls and how this impacted the cow, giving it a father complex before causing the cow to become a street walker. Just be happy you didn't order the fish. These guys can smell negativity a mile away, it is like a sixth sense to them. Give them a half a hour with Salma Hayek and she will come out of it looking like road kill. Seeing nothing but the negative is an art form to them.

Now, one of the questions I am asked about miserable assholes is, are they racist? Well, let's look at this a little further. See, with a miserable asshole, they are going to find so many other things to hate you for that race isn't really going to matter. To a miserable asshole, they are going to take the time to really get into your life, to see what all there is for them to low-rate you with. That's the great thing about these folks, no need to get offended over the race card, oh no, they go much deeper than that.

See, the key to focusing on the bad stuff is to preoccupy yourself with what's going wrong in a situation and ignore everything that could be seen as constructive or helpful. First and foremost, take all the positive aspects and discard them immediately. That way you have more time to dwell and contemplate on all the negative and bad stuff. Now what is great about this process is you get to create a lot of anxiety and fear along with a side of despair. And that goes a long way in getting to be a miserable asshole. Nothing better to get you miserable than to focus on the crappy stuff.

Don't ask a miserable asshole about the weather. Just don't do it, you'll be there for a half hour dying while forced to listen to how the weather is. You'll be kicking yourself for asking in the first place. Why? This is Why.

So, how's the weather? Mrs. Miserable Asshole, "It is so damn hot! Well, I've never. Did you know that my fat ass got stuck to my fine leather seat in my car. That is "Connolly" leather, not that cheap ass Nubuck leather that they use in a cheap old Ford, Oh, hell no. And to make matters worse, the detailing crew at the dealership didn't vacuum under those fine seats worth a damn, now my car smells like that Big Mac I bought the other day and dropped under the seat. didn't matter, whatever sauce they used tasted like vomit. I swear, they must go out of their way to hire morons. I think they took the change I had in the tray, you know you can't trust Mexicans, they will steal you blind. I mean I have one to do my house cleaning, everyone should have at least one even though she's a filthy bitch, she works cheap, looks like a little bowling ball but she's one of those good Mexicans. She said my name in Spanish is "Joder Perra." She said it meant Princess! Wished the hell she knew how to make a decent cup of coffee, every time she makes it, it taste like piss. Anyway, it is so hot that the sushi I bought at the store turned into fried fish by the time I got home, damn it's hot."

Okay, let's look at an another example of this principle at work. Let's take Joe and to just illustrate the point, say he just got fired, that's right, he lost your job. But not like he lost his car keys, because we both know that was a bullshit story to cover his ass for being late to work. No, this is the real deal Joe, You Got Fired!

What is interesting about getting fired is you are in a complete and utter disbelief in the fact that the "Man" would ever fire you. I mean, how is this company going to survive without you! Of course as the security guards are escorting you to the door, you realize that isn't a joke. As you are being thrown out onto the street, you ask for just one reason why they are shit canning your ass and you get the following response

1- You're always late, never on time.

2-You never do your job.

3-You're always sneaking off early.

4- You have way too many personal problems.

5- You drink on the job.

6-You smell.

7-You steal your co-workers lunch.

8-You're an Idiot.

9-You screw everything up that you touch.

10-You fart just to smell yourself and you stink!

At this point, you mention that you only ask for one reason, not a fucking book! About the time your keister is hitting the pavement the reality of getting fired starts to sink in along with some asphalt into your palms. About this time, you begin to focus on all the negative aspects of this event. Your mind begins to filter out the constructed bits and slowly starts to zero in on just the crappy stuff. Some would say that this is enough to make your day miserable. But let's play this out.

Time to take an inventory. Okay, you lost your job. That's okay, no wait a minute, your car is out of gas. That's bad. No, not really, with no job, there is no way to make the payments, so the car gets pick up. That's bad. No, not really, one less payment to worry about. Next, how are you going to feed the family? That could be bad, but wait, didn't your wife leave you in the last chapter? Yes, she did, and just in time too. So, that is something positive. You still have lotion so you can make do. Oh but there is dog food to buy, no, he left with her, remember? Okay, so far, there really isn't that much bad stuff to focus on. No job, no problem, get on unemployment and that takes care of the rent. Won't cover the lights but you've been living without lights for the last few weeks and cold showers are only once a week so you can maintain your lifestyle.

Why even bother to take a bath once a week? It is not like you have a job to go to anymore. Maybe you can pick up some food stamps, sell them to the family down the street and now you have beer money. What you thought of as being a really bad, crappy situation can turn out to be pretty good for you. And why is this important? Because you have more time to dwell on why you are such an idiot and why the "Man" is keeping you down.

The effects of focusing on the bad, the ugly, and the negative is it gives you the excuse to not care, not to have any self respect and to realize that it doesn't matter, you're a loser anyway. You've heard it your entire life and now it is coming to pass so why fight it. Life sucks and you're stuck in it with no way out. And this my friend, takes a lot of time and work, to just sit there and dwell on all the crappy stuff in your life.

The upside? Even in a silver lining lies a dark cloud. So don't worry, there is plenty to look for when you want to focus on the bad, negative and crappy stuff. Because of your lifestyle, there will be no shortage of shit for you to dwell over. If you're lucky, maybe it'll rain shit on you. By focusing on all of this you'll be able to come up with a lot more excuses and become even a bigger miserable asshole and have a goal to strive for, to become a self centered, self absorbed loser who's reason to live life is thinking that you are really important and matter. All of this while wallowing in your very own personal cesspool.

Isn't life grand?

CHAPTER FOUR-BEING A FORTUNE TELLER- PREDICTING YOUR CRAPPY FUTURE

Ah, this is where skill comes into play. Let's pick up where we left off in the last chapter. Our friend Joe, who lost his job, along with his car, wife, dog, lights, and whatever the finance company could get their hand on, is now at home with no job. So what does our friend begin to do? I'll tell you what he does, he starts to predict his future. Yes, he becomes a Fortune Teller. With his vast experience of knowing how to really fuck up a life, he feels justified in being able to predict his own future.

If you are not miserable enough by now, here is the key, it is to really get down and dirty. Yes, all it takes is to start basing your future off your past. What is the old saying that stock brokers use? "Past performance isn't an indicator for future results." But our friend has never heard this before so he looks at his past and thinks there is nothing he can do to change anything. Armed with this new found knowledge, he sits out on the front porch, surrounded with the necessary provisions to hunker down for the long haul. Yes, with enough beer, cigarettes, and chips, he can ride out this scenario to doomsday.

Misery loves to be fed and really loves to feed on fear, despair, hopelessness, and failure. With the right kind of food, misery can become a black hole, sucking up any hope of a life along with anything positive like joy, peace, happiness, and even love. Yes, misery has an appetite. Dwelling on how bleak the future is going to be will reinforce your misery into being the main stay of your life. It can lock you up and throw away the key because you have surrendered to your fate, because it has you believing it.

The downside to the law of attraction is it works no matter what you focus on. If you focus on impending disasters, then guess what, that is what you are going to get. Intention works regardless if it is positive or negative. In fact, I believe it works better when you focus on the negative aspects of life.

You seem surprise to be reading about Intention and the Law of Attraction in a book about miserable assholes. Well, why wouldn't it work for you? There is no rule that says it cannot help push you down into the cesspool if that is what you want contemplate.

This is the great thing about Intention and the Law of Attraction, it doesn't discriminate against the miserable losers out there. It honors them just like it honors the winners. So, keep on dwelling on how much worst life can be and it will deliver it to you on a silver platter, or least on a semi-clean paper plate.

Fortune telling is a form of self fulfilling prophecy. Let's return to our friend Joe. So here is Joe, sitting on the front porch, telling anyone and everyone he sees about his tales of woe. He weaves stories of grievous distress and his affliction to sorrow. Even the poor birds in the trees can't take it anymore and pack up and leave for brighter days. The squirrel after listening to him runs out in front of a passing car to end his troubles. The extant of Joe's stories affect everyone and everything around him, hell, even the weeds won't grow in his yard. Poor Joe is fast becoming a master at cultivating misery. If there was an award for the most miserable asshole, I am sure Joe would be nominated for it.

There he is, sitting on the front porch in his old worn out metal chair thinking about how he will never find another woman to put up with his crap. He thinks how he is destine to be alone because he has nothing to offer a woman. He reinforces this belief by not wanting to change his situation. Rather than change his fate, he subconsciously feels that he isn't worthy to a have a good woman. These feelings of being unworthy, of being inferior actually help fuel the misery by telling him he doesn't deserve nothing better than what he already has.

It is interesting that people like Joe are the ones that have their front yard in an unkempt state. You would think with all the time in the world, he would get up and clean the place up, mow the yard, repair the fence, maybe even put a coat of paint on the house. But no, misery loves company and it wants Joe to continue to sit in that chair and wallow in it.

Why is this so? Because when you live in misery, it is so much easier to sit there in that chair and blame everyone and everything for all your problems. It is easier to think that nothing matters, that nothing will ever change and worst of all, because you don't deserve any better.

The thing about Joe is he is ensured of a crappy future for no other reason than that is all that he thinks about. So, if you are wanting to keep your misery, to ensure that it never leaves, then take a lesson from Joe and dwell on it to the point that nothing but misery are the only thoughts you have.

CHAPTER FIVE-TAKING EVERYTHING PERSONAL

This is a reinforcement of the previous chapters. Because you think the world revolves around you, because you think that it is everybody else's fault that your life is in the toilet, that it will never change, it is natural for you to take everything personal. It is as if God himself has singled you out to shit on. You are so special that he, God himself has nothing better to do but to make your life a living hell. Again, here we go with the excuses. It isn't enough to blame everyone here on Earth, now we have to drag God into it.

In order for this to really work you have to stop believing that shit happens for no reason. Sometimes it snows in April because it just happens. But you refuse to believe it.

You've got to change everything around to where it happens to you because you are just an innocent victim and you are being singled out, by the Man and God. You haven't done anything to deserve any of this, that you just don't understand why it always happens to you.

No matter what happens, someone or something has it in for you. If a bird shits on you as you walk down the street, it is because the bird has got it in for you. Maybe because you ran off all of his friends with your non-stop complaining, moaning and bitching. Yeah, that's it, you are getting paid back for your suffering by getting shit on by a bird. Damn, Life is so unfair.

Taking everything personal is another way of getting out of taking responsibility for your own actions. What I mean by this is by blaming others for what you think is an injustice you get out of taking any responsibility. Like Joe, he blames the "Man" for losing his job. It isn't his fault that he was late to work, it isn't his fault he didn't grow up with a proper education, it isn't his fault he couldn't perform his duties at his job.

Instead, he blames everyone and feels that he is being singled out to be pick on because of his perceived lack of ability. Why does Joe feel he is being singled out? Because everyone is jealous of him. He knows that they all wish they could be like him, Mr. Cool.

Here is an example on why Joe thinks he is getting picked on. Joe drinks too much and over sleeps the next morning. He is late for his appointment at the unemployment office and doesn't get his benefits that week. Instead of assuming responsibility for his actions, he blames the person that is handling his claim for being an asshole. He blames the system for being insensitive to his needs. That they don't understand what he is going through. He couldn't make it on time, he doesn't have a car because he lost his job, the bus was running late and he had to get dressed. Excuses, excuses, excuses.

Not once does he realize that maybe these problems are the result of his drinking the night before with full knowledge that he had an appointment early in the morning and would need to take the bus to get there since he lost his car. The reason he lost his car was because of his lack of commitment to working at his job. That is the reason to most of his problems, a lack of commitment along with being unable to take any responsibility.

This is another effect of misery, it blinds you to the truth. Misery will always take the easy road, the path of least resistance. Misery doesn't believe in mirrors either, because it cannot handle seeing reality. But misery loves company, give Joe a 6-pack of beer and an audience and he is set to give a performance to all that will listen about his "woe is me" speech.

Taking everything personal creates a environment where you are looking for it. And if it isn't there, your mind will fabricate whatever it needs to find it. It is a combination of focusing on all the negative stuff, blame and thinking that everything is always it's all about you. It has to be all about you. It is having this sense of self-importance that brings it all together.

It is a twisted and warped logic that invents these thoughts fueled by a need to find a reason of why you are getting shit on. It is crazy how you can find fault even in a rain storm or a sunny day. There is no limit as to what you can take on a personal level. Even the girl at the gas station who smiled at you did it in a condescending manner. When taking everything personal, no one can do anything right nor will anything ever meet your satisfaction. Even the poor kid back in the kitchen cooking your hamburger has an agenda against you. {but he really does}

In order to be miserable, you have to disconnect from the real world, you cannot think that there might be more to life than just you, oh no, it has to be all about you, that there is a global conspiracy against you. In order to be miserable, you need to be a little insane to keep it going. Another word for you could be psychopathic asshole as this is how you are seen by the world. Either way, a miserable asshole loves shit, they just love it, even bathe in it, collect it and joins any shitface collecting club to ensure they stay on top of all the new shit coming out.

DENNIS WALLER

CHAPTER SIX-TAKING GUILT TRIPS

Whenever you are confronted with something that disagrees with you, you cop out by taking a guilt trip. When you feel neglected or no longer the center of attention, you'll go on a guilt trip. Guilt trips are your reset/default setting when you are losing your grip on the situation.

Let me give you an example. We know that Joe had a wife that left him. Her name is Beth. What we didn't know is that Beth enjoys being a miserable asshole too. Whenever she gets into the doldrums, she takes a guilt trip. Yep, straight down "Woe is me Boulevard." She would start off how her life is such a mess, how the bills never got paid, how she struggles with making ends met with Joe's drinking. How she did everything on her own with no help from anyone, thank you very much!

While these are facts, she enhances these facts and delivers them in a manner where people would feel sorry for her. She is a waitress at a local diner. And like Joe, she has her excuses of why she is always late. When the heat was coming down on her, she would get out of it by expressing all the woes that she was going through. Through pity, people let her slide, the customers would leave bigger tips. She realize that throwing a pity party, by having a guilt trip, people responded with love and kindness and more importantly, money.

It was when she enforced her sense of self-importance on these people by having a guilt trip that she felt power over them and fueling her sense of superiority. This deception is the worst kind. Taking advantage of others by making them feel sorry for you.

It reminds me of the little cat in the animated movie, "Puss n Boots." The voice of the little cat was played by Antonio Banderas. Every time Puss would get cornered, those big eyes would pop out and that sweet little smile would come across his face, all the while, his sword was being positioned to run you through as soon as you looked away.

Joe is good at guilt trips too. Just ask the landlord what he has to go through every time he goes to the house to collect the rent money from Joe. The landlords name is Henry. He tells his wife that he hates going over there because it wears him down to hear the same story over and over. He said that Joe must have a script by the way he delivers his sad song of woe. He also said by the time he leaves there he feels dirty and not even a hot shower will wash away the crap he had to endure while listening to Joe for a half a hour.

So what does Joe do with his guilt trip for his landlord to feel this way? Here is a little bit of it from what Henry has recalled.

"Hey Henry, what are you doing here? Ah man, don't tell me its rent time again. Man, you are not going to believe all the crap I've been through. I told you my wife ran out on me, yep, took every dime I had in the bank too. Not only that, she took anything that was worth having.

Oh, my car? Well, you see, I lost my job. Seems they don't understand what I am going through and you know that car lot wouldn't cut me any slack on the payments, they just wouldn't work with me on the back payments. I mean, I am a hard worker but how does anyone expect me to get a job without a car?

I am trying to put something together but those people down there at the unemployment office won't give me the time of day. Yeah, you know those buses never run on time and I misses my appointment but they wouldn't hear any of that, they just don't understand what I am going through here. Now I have to wait another two weeks to get an appointment with them, in the meantime, I am on my own. I don't have any family I can count on, I have no idea what their problem is, it's not like I am doing crack or anything anymore.

Yeah, the lights are still out. I was going to get them turned back on but with all these problems with my unemployment. Yeah, that's a case of beer on the front porch, but it's not mine, ah, a friend dropped it off. I am sober, have been now for three, four hours. How do you expect me to deal with this? I mean a man deserves a beer now and then. Ah, looking for a job? Well, I am planning on it, as soon as I get some clothes washed. Well, I can't do laundry until I get that check first, you know? "

What do you think Henry sees and hears when he goes to see Joe about the rent? Well, let's hear what Henry tells his wife,

"That lazy, no good for nothing, worthless piece of shit. No wonder his wife left him, no wonder he got fired. He is a filthy, stinking crack head. All that comes out of his mouth are lies. I wish to God I never rented to house to him. How in the hell am I going to get him out without him destroying the house? I never seen a man with so damn many excuses. This bastard has one for everything. It is amazing how nothing is ever his doing. And this is where my tax dollars are going? To support his sorry ass? What the hell am I going to do with him?"

When Henry leaves, Joe goes back to his beer on the porch thinking how clever he is with his guilt trip and how it worked, it got Henry out of his hair. So back to sitting in the old metal chair thinking about how the world continues to rain shit down on him. Rocking back and forth, thinking how no one will give him a chance, after all, that is all he wants. All the while wishing he still had his dog so he could kick him, "damn dog." According to Joe, It's not Joe's fault everything is fucked up. "Oh man, how did things get so messed up? I would be better off dead."

The ultimate goal for misery, death. At this stage, that is just about the only way out of the suffering and misery. So go ahead, die bastard die!

Well, this is one chapter that Joe won't be in too much. It's about thinking. This chapter is about over thinking things. Misery can't stand to be still. It always needs to be doing something. It will make the mind turn and turn. It cannot buy anything at face value, there's always a motive to everything. Over thinking is the process of placing too much emphases on ordinary situations. Because misery has to be fueled by the actions of others, it must create those actions even when no one has done anything.

Joe has an older brother and he is a miserable asshole too, his name is Seth. Now Seth is a little brighter than Joe and has a decent job as a warehouse manager. He isn't liked too much because he is the master at finding fault in everything done and always focusing on the negative aspects of the job.

One morning there was a breakdown in communication between the front office and the warehouse. Seth was called in to settle the dispute. During the ordeal, there was a lot of huffing and puffing with bad words being thrown around. On the way back to the warehouse Seth started to ponder on the events, let's take a look into Seth's head to see this over thinking at work,

" John said he didn't give a shit about the warehouse but Bob said he did give a shit. And when I told Jose about the problem, he said he wasn't going to take any shit from John or Bob. Thereafter, Juan said he was going to take a shit and left.

I don't understand Bob. Why would anyone want to give a shit? I mean, that's gross. Really man, think about it. Taking a shit in a bag and giving it to someone just because you want to give a shit? I don't get it, I am like John, I really wouldn't want to give a shit.

The only thing worse than giving a shit would be someone who would a take a shit. Oh My God! Don't tell me, is Juan going to the front office to take a shit from Bob? Man, that isn't right, it's downright sick, I work with a bunch of sick bastards, all they have on their mind is each other's shit, to hell with it, I am going on break and having another cup of coffee even though it taste like piss."

As you can see, Seth over thought the whole process of thinking about the issue at hand and missed the point completely. This is what being in a state of misery does to you. You are so focused on the shit happening that you miss all the good stuff going on in life. While Seth looks like a decent guy, his mind is filled with shit.

Let's take Joe sitting on the porch after the landlord left. While Joe feels clever because he thinks he pulled the wool over Henry's eyes, he still cannot stop thinking what Henry could be up to. So, for the rest of the night and case of beer, Joe will sit there thinking of all the different situations that he can think of. All of them against him. It seems that no matter what, the "Man" is out to get him. Which makes no sense since Joe hasn't done anything to deserve any of this.

When Joe isn't thinking about Henry, his thoughts turn to his wife. He thinks that there must be another man involved. He sits there in disbelief because he never did anything for her to leave him like that. He was a good husband and provider. At least according to him. So, it must be her, yeah, she must have someone else, that's it.

And that damn dog, just can't believe that the dog would run off too. Must be something wrong with the dog too. That dog was never quite right. Hell, it's a dog, if it gets hungry, it could have gone out and catch a rabbit or something. What the hell was wrong with him anyway. Must be another dog down the street somewhere. That must be it! Anyway, it doesn't matter, he was a stupid dumbass of a dog. A total moron of a dog. Better off without him.

Well, if only the dog could talk and in this story he can! His name is Rover and he has a story to tell about old Joe.

"And they call us dumb animals. Joe is the biggest dumbass I ever seen. He couldn't wipe his ass if his life depended on it. I never seen a human complain as much as he does. I never understood why Joe would sit there and drink all night. Hell, Joe played with his nuts more than I licked mine. And Joe's idea of a retirement fund is called a 401Keg. It is collecting all the empty beer cans and saving them for a rainy day. That's his Excuse for drinking, he has to contribute to his retirement fund. After listening to him all this time, you would think that the President calls him for advice since according to Joe, he knows more than anyone out there. I had to leave, it was getting where he was peeing on all of my trees and the smell, and they thought it was me. I was tired of being blamed for everything. I had to leave, I even went back to the pound and asked them if I could stay, they said no. Beth isn't any better, the way they drink, they should have been fish, except she brings me left over's from her job. And fuck Joe if he thinks I am going to go eat Hobby the rabbit, hell he is my friend, friends don't eat friends"

As you can see, not even the dog wanted to have anything to do with Joe.

And poor Seth, while at work he asked Mary in the front office what happen to an order that needed to get filled that he couldn't locate on his desk. He was told that it must have vanish into thin air because she couldn't find it either.

There goes Seth over thinking again, "Why is it always into thin air that things and people disappear in? Can't people and things disappear into fog, hot air, or maybe humid air? Why does it always have to be thin air? And why does my coffee always smell like urine and what is this sauce that looks like spit on my hamburger and what did Juan mean when he said, fuck this shit and went home, is he going to have sex with the brown paper bag of shit? And what's this nonsense about getting off Scot-free? Why is it the Scots and not the Irish or the Welsh? Why do the Scotts get off free and the rest of us have to pay"

On the way home Seth was excited to hear on the radio about the premier of a new show on TV. It is called, "Guess Who's Shit This Is!" Yes, in this show, the contestants all take a shit in an unmarked brown bag. Then the bags are all mixed up and the contestants are given a bag and have to guess who's shit it is! Seth is excited to learn more about taking and giving shit plus to learn who's shit is who so he may handle his shit at work better.

Let's leave Seth to figure that one out on his own. At least while he is over thinking something useless, he isn't getting on anyone's nerves.

On the subject of over thinking, ever notice it is the miserable assholes that call everyone else a miserable asshole? Maybe I am just over thinking here.

CHAPTER EIGHT-DESTROYING THE LIVES OF PEOPLE AROUND YOU

Yep, One measure you can use to see where you are on the Path to becoming a major league miserable asshole is by looking at the people around you and see how they react to you.

While at work, take notes of the physical and mental health of your co-workers, do the same at home and take notes about your family and friends, {God forbid you have any.} Now, let's take a look to see where you are.

Does any of your co-workers, family or friends display any of the following symptoms:

Your co-workers show tendencies to want to go into a fit of rage when you look or talk to them?

You have found them at times contemplating suicidal thoughts?

Have you notice that your co-workers got a group discount to attend "Concealed Handgun Classes?"

Have you heard the words, "murder and I'm going to kill him or her" behind your back?

When describing the overall attitude of your co-workers, would the words best used to describe them be Frustration and Exasperation?

Have you notice any of your co-workers buying 50 pound bags of Lime and shovels?

When a co-worker offers to bring back your lunch, there is a "mystery sauce on it that resembles spit or phlegm?

Does the coffee your co-worker bring you have a urine taste or smell to it or have some foreign substance floating on top?

Have you notice that in the office memos regarding a meeting, the time stated is always after the meeting ended and you missed it?

Is there an unusually high amount of medical claims for ulcers, or high blood pressure at work?

Does it seem that you are never invited to any social functions outside of work?

Has the locks on your car ever been filled with super glue?

Or all the toilet paper disappears from the restroom prior to you using it?

Have you ever been compared to General William Sherman on his march to Atlanta? Leaving nothing but scorched earth behind in your wake?

Has your name been used in the same sentence with names like Hitler, Stalin and Mussolini.

At home, your significant other always develops a case of the hives whenever you want to get close to them?

Or they seem to have a headache that never goes away when you are around?

Or when you touch her she says, "Don't touch me, you make me sick?"

Not even the dog will come up to you, much less eat your dinner, {because of the secret sauce?}

Do you notice that when people cough, it sounds a lot like "asshole?"

For some reason you always miss your kids soccer games because they forgot to tell you the right time or place?

That your car seems to have an abnormal amount of bird shit after being parked overnight?

Does your neighbors suddenly go inside when you go outside?

Does the paperboy always seem to throw your paper on the roof?

Have you notice that same mystery sauce on your food at home?

And that same taste or smell of urine in your coffee?

Do you get the same answer when you ask why, "Oh, it must be those bitter coffee beans?"

Do you notice that whatever line you get in at the grocery store, it closes as soon as you get in it?

When you go to the coffee shop for your morning coffee, it has the same taste as the coffee at home and work?

When you go into a fast food restaurant, the employees fight over who is going to not take your order?

And the same mystery sauce is on your burger?

The same mystery sauce no matter which restaurant you go to?

You go to a home improvement store and it turns into a ghost town?

When you pick up your clothes at the cleaners, they seem more dirty than they were before you brought them it?

Does the clerk behind the counter uses a language you don't understand while you are in the store? Even when the tone of their voice indicate severe hostilities, they say it's only a blessing?{because you are leaving}

Do Divorce Lawyers fight over your business before you even get married?

Every time you go to visit your friends, they are never home, even if you can swear that you seen them through the window?

Or when you go to visit your parents, the locks have been changed?

Your idea of deer hunting is running over your mother?

You sign up to be a organ donor and they tell you, "No Thanks!"

You go to sell your blood and they pay you to leave instead?

While at the store, you find it necessary to stop in the middle of the door, blocking everyone, so you may do an inventory of your purchase?

Or find it necessary to stop in the middle of said door to send a text or contemplate the meaning of life?

Your co-workers and family have your emails set to go straight to spam?

Your mail at work and home has a funny smell to it, kind of like your coffee and hamburger?

You try to get a subscription to "Better Living" and they tell you, "Not Possible."

You try to get a subscription to "Guns and Ammo" and instead you feel like you have a target on your back with all the gunshots fired at you?

You take your dog to the vet and he refuses to leave from there and go back home?

Or your dog runs away only to find out that he went back to the dog pound on his own accord?

That the dog asked to be euthanized rather than going back home with you?

When you go to the Pet Store, all the birds in the cages pretend that they are dead as to keep you from buying any of them?

Facebook will not even allow you to have a page? Or if they do, you have a negative 5 friends?

Or, you get a post on your page that says, "Die you miserable bastard, die!" and its from Mark Z?

And, on Myspace, they tell you, Not your space?

You go on Match.com and they match you with Donald Trump? And he won't have anything to do with you, your fired before ever getting hired?

As a kid, not even your imaginary friends would have anything to do with you?

Your wife or children tell you that they are going to get a job being a Turkish Customs Agent, because after living with you, seeing a bunch of new assholes would be refreshing?

Have you ever been asked to be the poster child for pro-abortion proponents? Or at schools, they use your photo as to why people should practice safe sex?

Is Bin-Laden your biggest fan on Myspace?

Do you get fan mail from Gitmo?

Have you been referred to as the Anti-Christ on TV by preachers?

Do you get thank you notes from local doctors for creating all the new business for them since to moved to town?

Are you extremely proud and relish in your own shitheadedness?

You take credit for the accomplishments of other people?

You really enjoy and are very quick to point out others' mistakes?

You really enjoy watching people suffer, especially when you are the cause of their suffering?

You always have time to stop and really enjoy the misery of other people?

Your Dream job is to be a collection agent for the IRS.

You cannot stand to see anyone do better than you or be told that they are doing a better job than you even if it is true?

Voted in your high school yearbook to be most likely either a serial killer or President?

Have you ever been invited to go camping and once you got there, there wasn't anything but a hole dug with a blanket and a brick waiting for you, along with that bag of Lime?

Not even Joe Pesci or Robert De Niro will mess with you?

After church service, you walk up to the priest and ask him if the Pope really shits in the woods?

Or when the priest smiles at you, you ask him, "What the fuck are you looking at?"

During the service, you let out a fart and laugh because you know no one will say anything?

You're the one that makes left hand turns from the far right hand lane?

You take the exit lane all the way to the end and then try to cut over just to piss off everyone?

You feel the need to have your front bumper attached to the car in front of you during rush hour traffic just to screw with the other driver?

You eat your bowl of cereal, talk on the phone and read the paper while driving?

And for women, all of the above plus putting on your makeup and hose?

Or, maybe you like to drive with the front seat in the back down so low that no one including you can see what the fuck you're doing?

You like rap so much that you feel compelled to have people in the next state hear it too, at 3 in the morning?

You like to cut into a funeral processions to save stopping at red lights, and then post it on your twitter account?

And you continue to the grave site to cruise for chicks? And asked if there is a wake with food available after the service?

On your death bed, the grim reaper comes to get you, takes one look at you and says, "fuck this shit" and lets you live?

You love watching Guy Ritchie's movie, "Revolver" because the psychopathic asshole character Ray Liotta plays in the movie was modeled after you?

Do you see any patterns developing here? If so, they are defensive mechanisms set up by the people and animals that you come in contact with to protect them from you.

The funny thing, you do not even realize the path of destruction you leave as you go through life. How many ulcers and heart attacks can be attributed to you?

In order to be truly successful as a miserable asshole you Must cause wide spread havoc and misery among everyone you come in contact with. Your presence alone is enough to negatively impact relationships, social functions, family reunions, work and home environments. Bring distress to all around you and single handedly create an environment that resembles an apocalypse.

You have your head so far up your ass that you cannot see how you are destroying the lives around you. If this is the case, then you are doing good as a miserable asshole and take solace in knowing that everyone around you knows what a miserable asshole you are! You're doing great!

CHAPTER NINE-YOU MUST BE CERTIFIED AS HAVING APD

To close out this book on becoming the most miserable asshole possible, I feel that you need a goal to aim for. Since there isn't a technical term yet for miserable assholes, I guess you will have to settle for being thrown into the complete asshole group. Which isn't bad because from all appearances, the general public can't tell you all apart anyway. So, to keep this simple we will use the criteria for APD. APD stands for Asshole Personality Disorder. APD is the most common mental disorder among humans. And for those of you who do not believe this is real, here is a website that will validate my findings,

http://uncyclopedia.wikia.com/wiki/Asshole_Personality_Disorder

Here is a list of the symptoms or character traits you must have in order to be certified as a bona fide miserable asshole. For those of you who score a perfect rating, please contact me and I'll personally send you your certificate so you may display it promptly for those who haven't figured it out by now. Or, maybe you know someone that is and wish to award them with a certificate. What a great gift idea for the ultimate miserable asshole. Just a thought.

Here is the list,

1-Suffering from being self-centered, self-absorbed, or being in a state of self-importance.

2-An inability to conform to any set of rules or protocols because you feel you are above everyone else therefore not subject to following rules. This is also an excuse for not having to take any responsibility for your actions.

3-Suffering from the belief that you actually know everything when in fact you are an idiot.

4-Suffering from the delusion that everyone is stupid and would benefit greatly if they would only listen to you.

5-Your value and belief system changes to fit the situation.

6-You are still able to walk around while having your head stuck up your ass.

7-Everyone around you suffers from headaches, high blood pressure, ulcers, or any other medical issue resulting from being in your presence.

8-You take great pride in your diplomatic skills, comparing yourself to people like Gandhi, Mother Teresa, Jesus, Buddha, or any other leading leader.

9-It seems everyone around you is a complete and bumbling idiot because their intelligence level is so far below yours. You feel like an Einstein among a bunch of monkeys.

10-You know that the universe revolves around everything you think or do.

In order to qualify for APD you must have at least 5 of the symptoms listed above. If you have less than 5, maybe being a miserable asshole isn't for you and you should seek out my other book, "9 Keys You Must Master to be Happy" cause being miserable and an asshole isn't working for you.

For those of you who scored higher, congratulations! And for those who scored a perfect 10, don't forget to send off for your "Master Certified Miserable Asshole" certificate.

My mailing address is: Dennis Waller, PO Box 210442, Bedford, TX 76095 and you can always email me at: dennismwaller@yahoo.com

For those who are in between, I would recommend reading this book again to see what areas you need to improve. Remember, if it is worth doing, then it is worth doing right. You have a goal and a map on how to achieve it. This book should serve you well in your quest in becoming the most miserable asshole there is.

There is one last favor I ask of you, please leave your thoughts in a review about the book here at Amazon Kindle, and please be honest along with staying away from me. I am sure I can handle whatever you have to say, after all, I wrote the book! I hope you have had some fun along the way while reading this book.

Love, Peace and Joy to you all, Love ya, Dennis

CHAPTER TEN-I'M SORRY FOR INSULTING THE MONKEYS AND DEAD PARROTS

To all the Monkeys out there let me say that there was no harm intended towards you. I apologize for any inconvenience that references made to you might have cause among you in your Monkey World. There was no mention that you are or ever were miserable assholes. Please forgive me for using you to illustrate a point, thank you, Dennis

Also, to the family of the squirrel, I am deeply sorry for your lost. But you must admit, it was for the best.

Now, there were no Parrots harmed in the making of this book, however, I am still sorry for the death of the Norwegian Blue that met a most disturbing and horrible death at the hands of a mad, a really mad monkey.

ABOUT THE AUTHOR

First, let me ask you to leave a review with your thoughts about this book. It is important to me to know what you think. I write these books to serve you and anything I can do to do that job better is a blessing, Thank You, Dennis

Feel free to contact me with any thoughts or questions at DennismWaller@yahoo.com

Printed in Great Britain
by Amazon

22605764R00046